careers in the

THEATER

Dennis Babcock and Preston Boyd

photographs by
Milton J. Blumenfeld

Lerner Publications Company
Minneapolis, Minnesota

LIBRARY OF CONGRESS CATALOGING IN PUBLICATION DATA

Babcock, Dennis.
 Careers in the theater.

 (An Early Career Book)
  SUMMARY: Briefly describes various careers with a theater, including those of playwright, actor, lighting designer, musical director, stage manager, publicity director, house manager, and costume designer.

  1. Theater as a profession—Juvenile literature. [1. Theater as a profession] I. Boyd, Preston, joint author. II. Title.

PN2074.B3   792'.0293   74-11907
ISBN 0-8225-0324-7

International Standard Book Number: 0-8225-0324-7   Library of Congress Catalog Card Number: 74-11907

Second Printing 1976

Would you like to work in the theater?

Watching people act out a story has always been an enjoyable and fascinating form of entertainment. Thousands of years ago, people sat around campfires and watched fellow tribe members act out the story of a dangerous hunt or a funny trick that had been played on someone. Today, we can see actors performing, or acting out, stories on television, in movies, or on a stage.

This book is about stage performances, or plays. When you attend a play at a theater, you are in the same room with the actors. They are performing the play especially for you.

Many people work together to create a play and to bring it to life on the stage. In this book you will learn about the work these people do.

PLAYWRIGHT

Playwrights are writers of plays for the stage. They get the ideas for their plays in several ways. They might write a play about an historical event, or about something that has happened in their own lives. They might write a play that is pure fantasy. No matter what kind of play they write, they want to entertain people and to make them think and feel.

Sometimes, a playwright works with plays that someone else has written. When these plays are very old or very long, playwrights adapt, or fix, them to suit modern theaters. When playwrights do this, they must be very careful not to change the original playwright's ideas.

All playwrights must know a lot about people and about how they behave. They also must listen to the ways people talk. Knowing people and language helps playwrights write believable plays.

ARTISTIC DIRECTOR

For each play that a theater presents, there can be a different play director. During rehearsals, play directors help actors to interpret a play and to create the characters. The play director also guides the planning of the costumes, stage scenery, lighting, and music for a production.

Each play director is responsible for one play. The artistic director, however, has total responsibility for all the plays that are staged at a theater. He or she chooses the play directors, as well as the actors, designers, and other artists who work at the theater.

Artistic directors want plays to be successful. They want people to enjoy the plays, and to come to other plays that the theater produces.

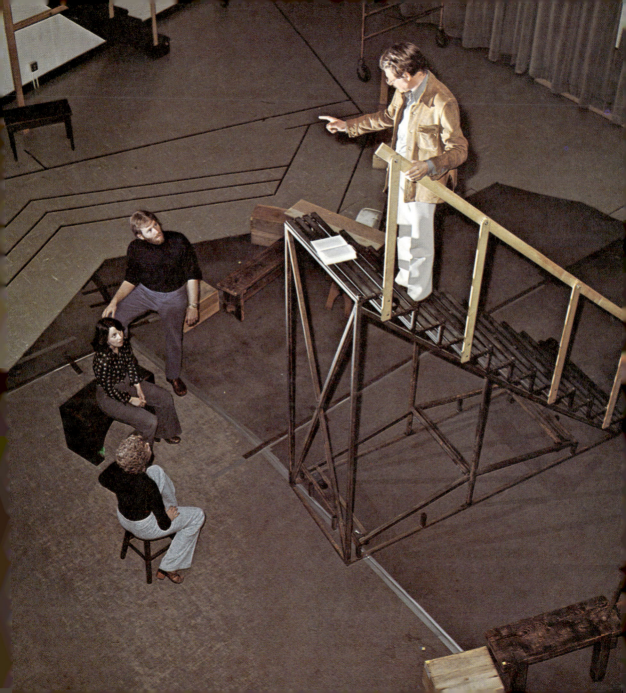

MANAGING DIRECTOR

The theater's business decisions are handled by the managing director, or producer. Part of the managing director's job is to control the money a theater raises. Some of this money comes from ticket sales and businesses, and some is given to the theater by individuals. With this money, the managing director prepares the budget for the theater. He or she makes sure that a theater doesn't spend more money than it receives. Salaries must be paid to the playwrights, actors, and other members of the staff. Also, different kinds of materials must be bought. Tickets and programs have to be printed, fabrics for costumes must be chosen, and supplies for the scene shop must be purchased.

The managing director plans ahead very carefully. He or she must be able to blend a knowledge of art with a knowledge of business to make the theater successful.

ACTOR

On stage, an actor is always pretending to be someone else. Using his or her own voice, body, intelligence, and the words of the playwright, the actor creates a character. For each play, the actor is a different character; that is, he or she plays a different "role." In order to make characters seem real, actors must have expressive faces, voices, and bodies. When a character in a play feels fear, or anger, or happiness, the actor expresses the feeling through his or her voice and body movements. Most actors also learn many skills in order to help them play their roles. These skills might include dancing, singing, or fencing (sword fighting).

Good actors can almost make us forget that we are at a play. As we watch them perform, we are taken into the world they are creating on the stage.

VOICE AND MOVEMENT COACH

An actor must be able to speak in a strong voice each time he or she performs. A voice coach teaches actors how to use their voices so that everyone in the theater can hear and understand clearly what is being said. The voice coach also teaches the actors how to use their voices without straining them.

The movement coach teaches actors how to stand, sit, and move on stage. Sometimes an actor has to play persons older than himself. The movement coach helps the actor to walk and move as an older person might.

Actors must also be able to stay relaxed as they move. The movement coach leads exercises to help them keep fit. The movement coach in the picture uses many kinds of exercises to prepare the actors for performances. Sometimes she teaches yoga (YO-gah), dancing, and karate (kah-RAH-tee).

COSTUME DESIGNER

The clothes that actors wear on stage are called costumes. Whether a play is set in ancient Greece or in present-day America, the costumes must be designed so that the actors look believable in their parts. The costume designer chooses the fabrics and colors for the costumes and decides how each character will look. He or she also chooses the wigs, jewelry, and shoes that the actors wear.

Costume designers are good researchers as well as creative artists. If a play takes place in a former time, the costume designer looks at old paintings to see how people dressed at that time. Then he or she uses imagination to make the costumes exciting and authentic.

Costume designers must know how to draw and sketch, so that they can show their ideas to other theater artists. The designers must also know how to make the clothes they design.

SCENE DESIGNER

When you see a play, one of the first things you notice is the stage scenery, or setting. The setting shows you where the action of the play is taking place. If the action takes place indoors, you might see a living room on the stage with windows, doors, furniture, and stairs. If the scene takes place outdoors, you might see trees, an old log, and a bright blue sky in the background. The scene designer plans all the stage settings. He or she must understand how the director wants to "stage," or present, the play.

A scene designer must be able to show his or her ideas to the director and to other theater artists. Therefore, a scene designer often draws or paints pictures of the settings. Sometimes a scene designer builds a small model of a setting. The scene designer in the picture is almost ready to take his model to the director for approval.

PROPERTY MASTER

Moveable objects used during a play are called properties, or "props." Hand props are objects the actor carries, like a sword or a flag. Set props, like tables or couches, are moveable but usually remain in one place. The property master is in charge of planning and building all these properties.

Some props, such as telephones and table lamps, are very common objects. Because they are like things we see every day, the property master will want these props to look very real. Other props, however, might represent odd things that we do not usually see, like a knight on horseback. These kinds of props do not have to be realistic. They often only suggest the items they represent. The prop in the picture is a horse. An actor can step into it and make it gallop with his own legs.

LIGHTING DESIGNER

When a play begins, the lights shining on the audience go off, and the special lights for the stage come on. The lighting designer decides how the stage will be lighted.

The lighting designer knows a great deal about electricity and complicated lighting equipment. He or she also knows what effects different colored lights will have on the faces of the actors and on the costumes they are wearing. The designer uses colored lights, and brightens or dims them, to set the mood of a play. Dim lights can make a tense scene seem more frightening. A happy scene becomes more jolly when bright lights shine onto the stage.

A lighting designer is one of the most important artists in a theater. In a sense, a lighting designer paints a picture using light as a paint and the stage as a canvas.

TECHNICAL DIRECTOR

Scene designers, property masters, and lighting designers plan how the stage will look during a performance. But their creative ideas would not work if there were no one to carry the plans through. The person who supervises the building of the settings and props, and who sets up the lights, is the technical director.

The technical director works in a special shop and oversees the workers who build the settings and props. Do you remember the model of the stage setting that the scene designer made? In this picture you can see that setting being built. The technical director is checking to make sure that his workers are following the scene designer's plans.

Technical directors keep track of all the settings, props, and lighting that are planned for a play. They make sure that these things are ready for a play's opening night.

MUSICAL DIRECTOR

Music is an important part of many plays. Like lighting, music helps set the mood of a play. The musical director, therefore, has a very important job. He or she decides what kinds of music should be used in a play.

Sometimes the musical director must write music especially for a production. Other times, the music for the play is already written. Then the musical director must teach it to the musicians who will play for the show. If an actor has to sing during the play, the musical director will help the actor learn the song. The musical director makes sure that the music for each show is played and sung in the most effective way.

The musical director is also an orchestra leader. He or she often conducts the orchestra during the performance of the play.

STAGE MANAGER

The stage manager is the assistant to the director of each play. With the director, the stage manager helps to decide on the rehearsal schedule. This schedule shows actors when and where their time is to be spent while they prepare for the play. Actors must know when to go to rehearsals, fittings for costumes, or special classes.

During rehearsals, the stage manager keeps a special script called a "prompt book." In it, the manager writes notes about where each actor is to move on stage, about cues for the lighting and sound, and about any changes in the script.

When the play is in production, the stage manager is the person in charge. He or she gives the "go ahead" to start each performance. The stage manager also gives the lighting and sound crew their cues during every performance.

PUBLICITY DIRECTOR

In order to see a play, people must buy tickets. The publicity director makes sure that the public knows when and where to buy these tickets. He or she also gives out information about the people who put on a play, and about the different plays that are to be performed. This information is sent to newspapers, radio, and television.

Sometimes the publicity director arranges tours through a theater. To teach the public more about the theater and its plays, the publicity director might also arrange for the theater staff to meet with business or social groups in the community.

Publicity directors want people in the community to know as much as possible about their theaters. They know that a living, self-supporting theater both educates and enriches the community it serves.

TICKET OFFICE MANAGER

The theater could not exist without an audience. The money that the people in the audience pay for tickets keeps the theater in business. The ticket office manager helps the business operation of the theater. He or she sees to it that people who want tickets to a play can buy them.

The ticket office manager must make sure there are as many tickets for each performance as there are seats in the theater. He or she can sell only one ticket for each seat. Some people buy a ticket in advance. This is called reserving a seat. When these people come to the ticket office or call on the phone, the ticket office manager helps them choose where they would like to sit.

Ticket office managers enjoy meeting and talking to many people every day. They are pleasant and helpful to all the theater's customers.

HOUSE MANAGER

The place where the audience sits to see a play is sometimes called "the house." The house manager makes sure that the audience sees the play in comfort. Before the play begins, the house manager stands in the lobby to welcome people to the theater. He or she works with the ushers to see that every ticket holder finds the correct seat. When everyone is seated, the house manager tells the stage manager that the play can begin.

The house manager in the picture is working with an usher to prepare for a large group coming to the theater. Both the house manager and the usher want to seat the group quickly and efficiently.

Theater careers described in this book

Playwright

Artistic Director

Managing Director

Actor

Voice and Movement Coach

Costume Designer

Scene Designer

Property Master

Lighting Designer

Technical Director

Musical Director

Stage Manager

Publicity Director

Ticket Office Manager

House Manager

A letter from a theater director

The Guthrie Theater

Dear Readers,

The theater is a wonderful place where we can go to laugh, cry, have fun, and learn more about ourselves and others. When you go to a play, you are in the same space as the actors, and you, the audience, are an important part of the story they are acting out for you on the stage. The actors are performing especially for you, sharing with you the thoughts and feelings of the characters they are playing.

As you read this book, you will also find out how many other people contribute their talents to the play you see on the stage. In an age when more and more things are being done by machines, it is important to tell ourselves that we, as human beings, belong to more than just our tiny moment in time. We are part of the past and our acts will shape the future. The contact between people and people, between actors and audience in a theater, can help us to understand our past and shape our future.

I hope you will go to the theater often and discover for yourselves the magic, excitement, and knowledge it can bring into your lives.

Sincerely,

Michael Langham

Michael Langham
Artistic Director

The publisher would like to thank The Guthrie Theater, Minneapolis, Minnesota, for its cooperation in the preparation of this book.

The photographs in this book realistically depict existing conditions in the service or industry discussed, including the number of women and minority groups currently employed.

We specialize in publishing quality books for
young people. For a complete list please write

LERNER PUBLICATIONS COMPANY
241 First Avenue North, Minneapolis, Minnesota 55401